from SEA TO SHINING SEA

South Dakota

By Dennis Brindell Fradin and Judith Bloom Fradin

CONSULTANTS

Herbert T. Hoover, Professor of History, University of South Dakota

Robert L. Hillerich, Ph.D., Professor Emeritus, Bowling Green State University;
Consultant, Pinellas County Schools, Florida

CHILDREN'S PRESS
A Division of Grolier Publishing
Sherman Turnpike
Danbury, Connecticut 06816

EL DORADO COUNTY FREE LIBRARY
345 FAIR LANE
PLACERVILLE, CALIFORNIA 95667

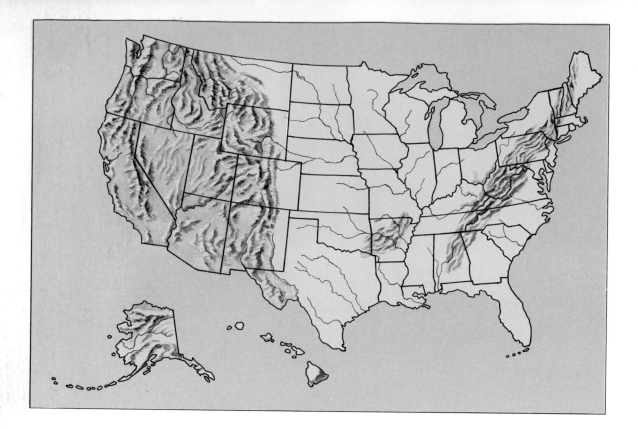

South Dakota is one of the twelve states in the region called the Midwest. The other midwestern states are Illinois, Indiana, Iowa, Kansas, Michigan, Minnesota, Missouri, Nebraska, North Dakota, Ohio, and Wisconsin.

For our cousins Sidney, Diana, and Robert Coleman and their remarkable mom, Aunt Syd

Front cover picture: The South Dakota State Capitol, Pierre; page 1: Fort Pierre National Grasslands; back cover: The Badlands at sunset, Badlands National Park

Project Editor: Joan Downing
Design Director: Karen Kohn
Typesetting: Graphic Connections, Inc.
Engraving: Liberty Photoengraving

Library of Congress Cataloging-in-Publication Data

Fradin, Dennis B.
　South Dakota / by Dennis Brindell Fradin & Judith Bloom Fradin.
　　p.　cm. — (From sea to shining sea)
　Includes index.
　ISBN 0-516-03841-9
　1. South Dakota—Juvenile literature. I. Fradin, Judith Bloom. II. Title. III. Series: Fradin, Dennis B. From sea to shining sea.
F651.3.F69　1995
978.3—dc20

94-43043
CIP
AC

Table of Contents

A boy feeding a wild burro in Custer State Park

Introducing the Sunshine State 4

Land of Infinite Variety 7

From Ancient Times Until Today 13

South Dakotans and Their Work. 29

A South Dakota Tour 33

A Gallery of Famous South Dakotans. 47

Did You Know? 54

South Dakota Information. 56

South Dakota History. 58

Map of South Dakota 60

Glossary 61

Index. 63

Introducing the Sunshine State

South Dakota is a big state in the midwestern United States. It was named for the Dakota, or Sioux, Indians. In the Sioux language, *Dakota* means "friends." Its name fits the friendly state well. South Dakota is known for its low crime rate. It is also known for its clear, sunny skies. One of its nicknames is the "Sunshine State."

South Dakota has a rich past. Lewis and Clark explored its land. Gold discoveries in the Black Hills attracted many people. Two of them were Wild Bill Hickok and Calamity Jane. Sitting Bull and Crazy Horse fought for Indian rights to the Black Hills.

Today, South Dakota is a farming leader. The state ranks first at growing oats and rye. Each year, millions of people visit the state. They enjoy South Dakota's beautiful and historic sites.

The Sunshine State has even more to boast about. Where are four presidents' faces carved onto

Florida is also nicknamed the Sunshine State.

4

a mountain? What state has the most buffalo? Where is the world's oldest continuously run gold mine? Where is the Corn Palace? The answer to these questions is: South Dakota!

Overleaf: The Falls of the Big Sioux River

5

Land of Infinite Variety

Land of Infinite Variety

S outh Dakota covers 77,116 square miles in the Midwest. Six states border South Dakota. To the north is its "twin," North Dakota. Minnesota and Iowa are to the east. Nebraska lies to the south. Wyoming and Montana are to the west.

"Land of Infinite Variety" is another South Dakota nickname. That's because the state has many kinds of landforms. Low, rolling prairies lie to the east. The Great Plains cover most of the west. Buttes rise sharply above the plains. These are steep, flat-topped hills. Deep, steep-sided valleys called canyons cut into the plains. The Badlands also mark the plains. There, wind and water have carved soft rocks into strange shapes. Farther west stand mountains called the Black Hills. There, Harney Peak rises 7,242 feet above sea level. This is South Dakota's highest point. It is also the highest point in the United States east of the Rocky Mountains.

Water, Woods, and Wildlife

South Dakota has nearly 300 natural lakes. Big Stone Lake and Lake Traverse are the largest ones.

The Badlands at sunrise

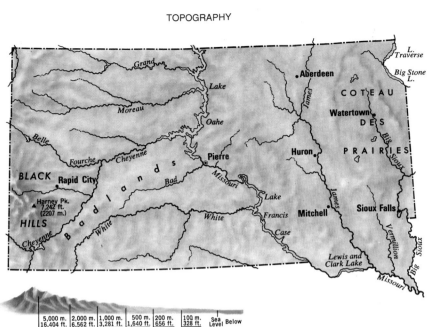

The state also has four big artificially made lakes: Oahe, Francis Case, Sharpe, and Lewis and Clark. These lakes are called the "Great Lakes of South Dakota." Dams built on the Missouri River formed them. Lake Oahe covers nearly 600 square miles. It is the state's largest lake.

The Missouri is the state's main river. "Big Muddy" enters South Dakota midway along the northern border. It winds to the state's southeast corner. Other major rivers flow through South Dakota: the Big Sioux, Vermillion, James, Grand, Moreau, Cheyenne, and White rivers.

Few trees grow in South Dakota. It is one of the least wooded states. However, spruces, junipers,

Left: King and Queen rocks along the Big Sioux River, Palisades State Park

9

A Pronghorn (above) can reach speeds of up to 60 miles per hour. Prairie dogs are members of the squirrel family. Coyotes are known for their sad howl.

Golden eagle

and pines cover the Black Hills. From far away, the green trees look black. Oaks, maples, willows, and ashes are other South Dakota trees. The state flower is the American pasqueflower. It is known for its purple blossoms. Other wildflowers include black-eyed Susans, forget-me-nots, and lady's slippers.

Bighorn sheep and Rocky Mountain goats climb around the Black Hills. Pronghorns run through the state. Prairie dogs burrow beneath the earth. They bark when chased by coyotes and badgers. The coyote is the state animal. South Dakota is sometimes called the Coyote State. White-tailed deer live in many parts of South Dakota. The country's largest buffalo herd lives there, too. The ring-necked pheasant is South Dakota's colorful state bird. Bald eagles and golden eagles fly about the state. The walleye is the state fish. Northern pike, bass, and bluegills also live in South Dakota waters.

CLIMATE

South Dakota is hot in the summer and cold in the winter. Summer temperatures often top 90 degrees Fahrenheit. Winter temperatures often dip below 0 degrees Fahrenheit. The state holds several records for fast temperature changes. On January 10, 1911,

Rapid City's temperature fell 47 degrees Fahrenheit in 15 minutes. On January 22, 1943, the temperature rose 49 degrees Fahrenheit in Spearfish. That happened in two minutes!

Windblown snowstorms called blizzards sometimes strike South Dakota. Long dry spells also hit the state. These are called droughts. Yet floods often cover parts of South Dakota. On June 9, 1972, over 6 inches of rain fell around Rapid City. The Canyon Lake Dam collapsed. At least 236 people were killed. Tornadoes often hit the state. These powerful whirling windstorms damage crops and buildings. They can also kill people and animals.

The Badlands in winter

11

The Stoneboat, *by South Dakota artist Harvey Dunn, shows a pioneer couple clearing huge stones from their fields so they can plant crops.*

From Ancient Times Until Today

From Ancient Times Until Today

Millions of years ago, dinosaurs roamed across South Dakota. Fossil bones of triceratops, Tyrannosaurus rex, and apatosaurus have been found there. South Dakota was also home to the archelon. It was the largest turtle of all time. Archelon measured over 11 feet long.

American Indians

The first people reached South Dakota about 10,000 years ago. These early Indians hunted big game such as mammoths. About 2,000 years ago, woodland people came to eastern South Dakota, where they began to raise crops and gather natural food. They also hunted game. Bones, tools, and pottery have been found. The tools show that these people mainly hunted for their food.

By the 1700s, three main Indian groups lived in South Dakota: the Arikara, Cheyenne, and Sioux. The Arikara were farmers. They lived along the Missouri River. The Arikara grew corn, beans, squash, and pumpkins. Their homes were made of

Prehistoric dinosaur skeletons at the Museum of Geology in Rapid City

logs covered by dirt. Many Cheyenne lived near the Black Hills. They traded horses to the Arikara for food crops. The Cheyenne used their horses to hunt buffalo. They carried their homes with them. These were buffalo-skin tents called tepees. The Sioux arrived around 1750. They traded with the Arikara for horses. Like the Cheyenne, the Sioux lived in tepees. They also hunted buffalo with bows and arrows. By the 1780s, the Sioux were the masters of the northern Great Plains.

A Brulé Sioux tepee village

Explorers and Traders

In 1682, explorer René-Robert Cavelier, Sieur de La Salle, claimed a huge piece of America for France. He named this land Louisiana. All of present-day South Dakota was included. La Salle never saw South Dakota, however.

Not until 1743 did non-Indians enter South Dakota. They were François and Louis-Joseph La Vérendrye. The La Vérendrye brothers came from Canada. They were looking for a water route to the Pacific Ocean as well as for trade. Near present-day Fort Pierre, they buried a metal plate. It further claimed the land for France.

The furs were used to make clothing.

The La Vérendryes opened South Dakota to French fur traders. These traders brought pots, pans, and tools for the Indians. In exchange, the Indians traded animal skins and furs. In 1762, France turned over its Louisiana lands to Spain. This included South Dakota. Yet, most fur traders in South Dakota were French. One of them was Pierre Dorion. He became South Dakota's first white settler. Around 1775, Dorion married a Sioux woman. They settled near present-day Yankton.

In 1800, France once again owned Louisiana, including South Dakota. By then, only about thirty non-Indians were in the region. Three years later, the United States bought French Louisiana. The Louisiana Purchase cost $15,000,000. Later, all or part of fifteen states were carved from this land. All of South Dakota was included.

President Thomas Jefferson sent Meriwether Lewis and William Clark to the new land. In 1804, the explorers traveled up the Missouri River into South Dakota. They reported that the land had plenty of fur-bearing animals. More fur traders arrived. Joseph La Framboise began a trading post in 1817. His outpost was South Dakota's first lasting non-Indian settlement. Later it was called Fort Pierre. In 1831, the fort was named for another fur trader, Pierre Chouteau, Jr.

Fort Pierre as it looked in the 1880s

Pierre Chouteau's steamboat, the *Yellowstone*, traveled to Fort Pierre in 1831. It was the first Missouri River steamboat to go that far north. The steamboats brought food and tools for fur traders. The boats carried furs from South Dakota. By the 1850s, however, the fur-bearing animals had been overhunted. Interest in the fur trade ended.

HOMESTEADERS, GOLD MINERS, AND INDIAN WARS

In the 1850s, thousands of Americans were looking for farmland in the West. South Dakota's Sioux sold their eastern land to the United States government. This opened South Dakota to farmers and towns-people. Sioux Falls was settled in 1856. Yankton was begun in 1859. The United States government formed the Dakota Territory in 1861. It included North and South Dakota and part of Wyoming and Montana.

To help the settlement of the West, Congress passed the Homestead Act (1862). It offered settlers 160 acres of free land. They had to live on and work the land for five years. Then, they would own it. By 1870, South Dakota had almost 12,000 non-Indian settlers. On the treeless prairie, homesteaders

cut chunks of sod into bricks. They used these bricks to build sod houses. These pioneers grew wheat and corn. The first railroad came into South Dakota in 1872. Even more people took trains to the territory.

In the 1860s, miners crossed western South Dakota. They were part of the Montana gold rush. In 1866, the army tried to build a road to the goldfields. It would have crossed Sioux land in South Dakota, Montana, and Wyoming. From 1866 to 1868, the Sioux attacked the soldiers. Chief Red Cloud led them. The Laramie Treaty ended Red Cloud's War in 1868. The Sioux were made a

This original homesteaders' sod house in Philip has been preserved.

Chief Red Cloud

Members of this army expedition found gold in the Black Hills in 1874.

promise. The Black Hills region would be theirs to keep as long as they wished.

To the Sioux, the Black Hills were holy ground. In 1874, an army expedition led by George Custer found gold there. Thousands of white people poured into the Black Hills. In 1875, the town of Custer was laid out. That was near the first gold strike. Far richer gold strikes were made north of Custer. There, in 1876, the gold-mining towns of Deadwood and Lead were founded. Gold drew 25,000 people to Deadwood in a few months. It became a "Wild West" town. Wild Bill Hickok was killed while playing poker in a Deadwood saloon. On August 2, 1876, Jack McCall shot him from behind.

To regain their land, the Sioux attacked many mining camps. Sioux leaders included Sitting Bull, Crazy Horse, and Gall. On June 25, 1876, they won the Battle of the Little Bighorn. This Montana battle is also known as "Custer's Last Stand." George Custer and more than 200 of his men were killed. In September, the army fought in South

Sioux leader Gall

Deadwood in 1876

Deadwood in 1876

Dakota against the Sioux. This is called the Battle of Slim Buttes. In October, the Sioux gave up some of their western lands. That included the Black Hills. Crazy Horse was killed. Most Sioux were pushed onto reservations after 1889.

Ranchers moved their cattle and sheep into western South Dakota. At first, the meat was sold to miners in the Black Hills. Then, railroads shipped the cattle to markets in Chicago.

In 1890, the government feared another Sioux uprising. On December 15, Sitting Bull was to be

Nearly all of these Sioux Indians were killed at Wounded Knee Creek only a few months after this picture was taken.

arrested. Instead, he was killed. His followers joined Chief Big Foot's Sioux near Wounded Knee Creek. On December 29, soldiers began firing at these Sioux. Nearly 300 Sioux were murdered at Wounded Knee Creek. This ended the fighting between whites and Indians in South Dakota.

SUCCESSES AND STRUGGLES OF THE YOUNG STATE

The year before the Wounded Knee Massacre, South Dakota became a state. Early in 1889, Congress divided Dakota into North Dakota and South Dakota. That November 2, President Benjamin Harrison signed both Dakotas into state-hood. President Harrison covered the names on the statehood papers. Then he shuffled them. Not even he knew which Dakota was made a state first. But *n* comes before *s* in the alphabet. So North Dakota is the thirty-ninth state. South Dakota is the fortieth state. Pierre (pronounced Peer) became South Dakota's capital. Arthur Mellette was the first state governor.

In the summer of 1889, a drought hit South Dakota. It lasted until 1897. This dry period helped cause the "Great Dakota Bust." Few new farmers arrived. Some already there packed up and left.

Benjamin Harrison

In the 1900s, wheat became South Dakota's most important crop. In 1917, the United States entered World War I (1914-1918). South Dakota provided wheat for the war effort. About 32,000 South Dakotans served in the war. Many of them were part of the 147th Field Artillery Regiment. This group won many awards for bravery.

In the 1920s, prices for farm crops dropped. The value of farmland fell, too. Some South Dakota farmers lost their farms. Then, the Great Depression (1929-1939) hit the country. Factories and banks closed. Workers lost their jobs. In the 1930s, another drought hit South Dakota. Crops died. Strong winds caused dust storms across the state. Billions of grasshoppers also destroyed crops. By 1935, 70,000 of the state's 85,000 farms had crop failures.

The government ran programs to help people survive the depression. Many South Dakotans planted trees in the Black Hills. Others built schools and roads. The government also raised the price of gold. That helped Black Hills mines.

World War II (1939-1945) helped end the depression. The United States entered the war in 1941. More than 64,000 South Dakota men and women served in uniform. South Dakota meat, milk, and wheat helped feed soldiers and sailors. Air

This South Dakota farmer's crops were ruined by the drought that hit in the 1930s.

Force bases were built near Sioux Falls and Rapid City. Joe Foss from Sioux Falls shot down thirty-one enemy airplanes. For this, he earned the Congressional Medal of Honor. Later, Foss became governor of South Dakota (1955-1959).

RECENT GROWTH AND PROBLEMS

The Pick-Sloan Missouri Basin Program (1944-1966) built four dams in South Dakota. The dams help control the Missouri River. They prevent floods. They also direct water to farmers' fields. The dams' power plants bring electricity to many farms. Behind each dam is a huge lake. They are called the "Great Lakes of South Dakota." These lakes are used for swimming, fishing, and boating. South Dakota's "Great Lakes" attract many tourists. Throughout the twentieth century, tourism has been a big South Dakota business.

Gavins Point Dam (above) formed Lewis and Clark Lake, one of the "Great Lakes of South Dakota."

South Dakota's cities grew during the 1980s. Rapid City's population rose from 46,500 to 54,500. Citibank moved its credit card headquarters to Sioux Falls in 1981. This brought thousands of jobs to the city. Sioux Falls' population grew by 20,000 between 1980 and 1990. Deadwood started booming again in 1988. That year, South Dakota legalized gambling. Dozens of gambling houses opened in Deadwood. Many jobs were created. The state gained millions of dollars in taxes.

Meanwhile, South Dakota farmers were having hard times. Farm costs rose in the 1980s. But farmers' earnings didn't. In 1980, the state boasted 68,000 farms. Only 35,000 remained by 1990. A hard drought in 1988 destroyed millions of dollars in crops. South Dakota Indians have also suffered. Joblessness is a big problem on the reservations. On the Pine Ridge Reservation, less than half the youths finish high school. Two-thirds of the adults have no jobs. In 1973, 200 armed Indians took over Wounded Knee. They held the place for seventy-one days. The Indians wanted more self-government on the reservations. They also hoped to gain back some western lands. Two years later, the Self-Determination Act for Native Americans was passed. Now, Indians on reservations can govern themselves.

The Sioux won another victory in 1979. The United States Court of Claims made a ruling. It said that the Black Hills had been stolen from the Sioux. The United States government offered them more than $100 million in payment. But the Sioux refused. Instead, they want their land back. They continue to work for this.

With interest, the government's offer for the Black Hills totaled nearly $400 million by 1994.

In 1988, gambling on reservations also became legal. Thousands of tourists gamble at casinos on the reservations. Many Indians now work in the casinos.

Governor George S. Mickelson declared 1990 the "Year of Reconciliation." He set up a group to work for harmony between white people and Indians. In 1992, *Money* magazine named Sioux Falls "The Best Place to Live in America." In 1994, the state's corn and soybean crops reached an all-time high. South Dakotans see these events as signs of good times ahead for their state.

In 1994, South Dakota's corn crop reached an all-time high.

Overleaf: A young Sioux dancer in traditional costume takes part in a presentation at Crazy Horse Memorial.

27

South Dakotans and Their Work

South Dakotans and Their Work

South Dakota's population is 696,004. Only five states have fewer people. More South Dakotans live in rural areas than near big cities. Most other states have more people living near cities.

Nine of every ten South Dakotans are white. Most of their families came long ago from Germany, Norway, and Ireland. South Dakota is home to 5,000 Hispanics. Most of their Spanish-speaking families came from Mexico. About 3,000 Asians and 3,000 black people live in the state. South Dakota is home to more than 50,000 American Indians. Most of them live on nine Indian reservations in the state. The Sioux make up the state's largest Indian group.

Above: Czech Days, in Tabor
Below: A boy at the Black Hills Rodeo

South Dakotans at Work

By 1994, more than 350,000 South Dakotans had jobs. About 85,000 of them are service workers. They include health-care workers and people who serve tourists. In 1974, the country's first Super 8 Motel opened in Aberdeen. Today, more than 1,100 Super 8 Motels stand in the United States

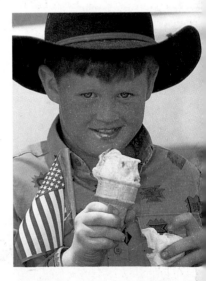

and Canada. Aberdeen is still headquarters for this motel chain.

About 85,000 South Dakotans sell goods. The items range from food in grocery stores to tractors. The Sunshine State has almost 70,000 government workers. Some work on Indian reservations or in national forests and parklands. Nearly 20,000 South Dakotans are in banking and related fields. Citibank is in Sioux Falls. It is the world's largest issuer of bank credit cards.

South Dakota has some of the world's best farmland. About 40,000 South Dakotans raise crops and livestock. They lead the country at growing oats and rye. South Dakota farmers are second at harvesting honey, sunflower seeds, and flaxseed. They are among the top ten hay, barley, wheat, and

Left: A rodeo rider at the Central State Fair, Rapid City
Right: Harvesting soybeans

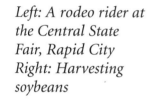

sorghum growers. They are also among the top ten beef cattle, sheep, and hog raisers.

Making products employs about another 40,000 South Dakotans. Packaged foods are the leading goods. They include meat, milk, flour, and animal feed. Machinery places second among the state's manufactured goods. The machines include farm equipment and grain elevators. Jewelry is made from Black Hills gold. Medical instruments and hot-air balloons are made in South Dakota, too.

About 2,000 South Dakotans work in mining. Gold is the state's top mining product. Only Nevada and California mine more gold than South Dakota. Oil, natural gas, and mica are other South Dakota mining products.

The annual Sioux Falls Balloon Rally attracts tourists to the area.

Overleaf: Mount Rushmore National Memorial

31

A South Dakota Tour

A South Dakota Tour

Millions of people visit South Dakota each year. They come to explore the natural wonders of the state, including the Black Hills and the Badlands. They also come to see its many Indian and pioneer sites.

Eastern Borderland Attractions

Sioux Falls is a good place to start a tour of South Dakota. This southeastern town was founded in 1856. It grew around a waterfall on the Big Sioux River. Today, Sioux Falls is South Dakota's largest city. More than 100,000 people live there.

The Siouxland Heritage Museums are in Sioux Falls. A restored 1890s courthouse is one of the museum buildings. The 1889 Pettigrew Home is the other building. Richard Pettigrew was South Dakota's first United States senator. Many visitors enjoy Sioux Falls' Great Plains Zoo. Its penguin pool is a children's favorite.

Northeast of Sioux Falls is Devil's Gulch. It is a 20-foot-wide, 50-foot-deep canyon. In 1876, Jesse James was fleeing from a posse. The well-known

Tourism is a giant business in South Dakota. About 8 million people visit there each year. That's eleven times the state's population.

A two-year-old lesser (red) panda at the Great Plains Zoo in Sioux Falls

34

Sioux Falls

bank robber jumped his horse across Devil's Gulch. He got away. A bridge now crosses the canyon. Nearby is Palisades State Park. Its tall red and purple rocks look like ruins of an old palace.

Madison is northwest of Sioux Falls. It is home to Prairie Village. Forty 1890s buildings were rebuilt there. They include a sod house and a wooden church.

Brookings is farther north. Founded in 1879, it is now the state's fifth-largest city. South Dakota

35

A steam traction engine at the State Agricultural Heritage Museum in Brookings

State University is in Brookings. With about 9,500 students, it is the state's largest school. Brookings is home to the State Agricultural Heritage Museum and the South Dakota Art Museum. Paintings by Oscar Howe and Harvey Dunn hang there. They are two well-known South Dakota artists. McCrory Gardens is also in Brookings. The Children's Maze is one of its many gardens. This 1,100-foot maze winds in many directions. Children have fun finding their way out.

De Smet is west of Brookings. This town is Laura Ingalls Wilder's *Little Town on the Prairie*. Wilder grew up there. Later, she wrote nine Little

House books. Today, her De Smet home can be toured. Each summer, De Smet hosts the Laura Ingalls Wilder Pageant. In it, actors perform stories from her books.

Watertown is north of Brookings. It is South Dakota's fourth-largest city. Watertown was home to South Dakota's first governor. His home, Mellette House, is open to the public. Close to town are Lakes Pelican and Kampeska. People hunt for geese and fish in their waters. Milbank is farther north. American Legion baseball was first played there in 1925. Today, about 80,000 people play "Legion ball."

The Laura Ingalls Wilder house in De Smet

Across Northern South Dakota

Sisseton is in the state's northeast corner. The Tekakwitha Fine Arts Center is there. This center has more than 200 works by Sioux artists. To the west is Roy Lake State Park. The lake was formed years ago by a melting glacier. Today, people catch their limit of walleye and bass at the lake.

West of Roy Lake is Aberdeen. With 25,000 people, it is South Dakota's third-biggest city. Wylie Park is a favorite spot for children. A zoo, a water slide, and a lake offer much fun. Storybook Land is

Storybook Land, in Aberdeen

there, too. Cinderella can be seen with her coach. Humpty Dumpty sits on his wall. Jack and Jill climb their hill. The park also has the Land of Oz. Visitors can follow the Yellow Brick Road to the Emerald City. L. Frank Baum is the author of *The Wonderful Wizard of Oz.* He wrote the book after moving from Aberdeen.

Ordway Prairie is in the middle of northern South Dakota. It is 12 square miles of grassland. Its grasses are the kinds South Dakota had before white settlement. Buffalo graze on the grasses.

Mobridge is farther west. This town's Scherr-Howe Arena has ten Oscar Howe murals. They show Sioux life. West of Mobridge are two huge Sioux reservations. Sitting Bull's grave is on the Standing Rock Reservation. The Cheyenne River Reservation has the Sioux Cultural Center. It is a good place to learn about Sioux history. Each fall at Eagle Butte, the reservation hosts a fair and rodeo. Sioux foods, dances, and stories are shared.

Far to the north is Lemmon. Petrified Wood Park is there. Long ago, minerals in water turned this wood to stone. Now, millions of pounds of petrified logs have been arranged in outdoor displays. Many pointed logs were used to build a fairy-tale castle.

The town of Buffalo is in northwestern South Dakota. In 1994, a Tyrannosaurus rex skeleton was found nearby. This dinosaur was about 40 feet long. It weighed nearly 16,000 pounds. Skulls from six triceratops have also been found there.

WESTERN SOUTH DAKOTA

The center of the fifty states is near Castle Rock. To the south is Belle Fourche. The Center of the Nation Visitor Center is there. The town is also home to the Tri-State Museum. Displays about the

Petrified Wood Park, in Lemmon

early history of South Dakota, Montana, and Wyoming are there.

South of Bell Fourche is the Black Hills town of Lead. The Homestake Gold Mine in Lead was begun in 1876. It is the world's oldest continuously run gold mine. The Homestake is also North America's largest working underground gold mine. The mine extends 1.5 miles below the Black Hills. Visitors can learn about gold mining at Lead's Black Hills Mining Museum.

Nearby is Deadwood. This old gold-mining town has been restored. Many buildings look like they did in the 1870s. The No. 10 Saloon is where

Left: The town of Lead (pronounced "Leed")
Right: The surface workings of the Homestake Gold Mine in Lead

Wild Bill Hickok was shot. He and Calamity Jane are buried at Deadwood's Mount Moriah Cemetery. Deadwood's Adams Memorial Museum has many items from the gold-rush days.

Rapid City is southeast of Deadwood. With 55,000 people, it is South Dakota's second-largest city. The Museum of Geology is in Rapid City. Fossils from Black Hills dinosaurs and other animals can be seen there. Rare minerals from around the world are also on display.

Southwest of Rapid City stands Mount Rushmore. There visitors can view the 60-foot-tall

Above: The restored downtown area of Deadwood is a National Historic Landmark.
Below: An actor costumed as Wild Bill Hickok

The model of the Chief Crazy Horse Memorial in the foreground shows how the finished sculpture on the mountain in the background will look.

heads of four presidents: George Washington, Thomas Jefferson, Theodore Roosevelt, and Abraham Lincoln. Some people view Mount Rushmore by helicopter. Nearby is another huge sculpture on a mountain. The Crazy Horse Memorial will show the Sioux chief on horseback. Korczak Ziolkowski began this work in 1948. When finished, it will be the world's largest sculpture. The entire figure will be 563 feet high and 641 feet long.

To the east is Custer State Park. One of the world's largest buffalo herds roams there. About 1,500 buffalo are in the herd. Harney Peak is just north of the park. In the 1920s, visitors rode burros up to South Dakota's highest peak. Descendants of those burros now live in Custer State Park.

Jewel Cave and Wind Cave lie beneath the Black Hills. They are among the world's ten longest caves. Jewel Cave was named for the shiny crystals on its walls. Wind Cave was named for strong winds that blow at its entrance. Some Wind Cave formations look like popcorn and frost.

Hot Springs is south of the caves. About 26,000 years ago, many mammoths sank into the ground. The bones of forty-eight mammoths have been dug up at Hot Springs. They are at the Mammoth Site.

SOUTHERN AND CENTRAL HIGHLIGHTS

Early travelers found parts of southwest South Dakota hard to cross. They called it the "badlands." Today, Badlands National Park covers 400 square miles. Odd-shaped hills, cliffs, and canyons are in the park.

The town of Wall is at the park's western edge. Wall Drug is the world's largest drugstore. But it's really a restaurant, gift shops, museum, and drugstore. Kadoka is east of Badlands National Park. Visitors enjoy Kadoka's Badlands Petrified Gardens.

Ice Age mammoth fossils have been dug up at Mammoth Site in Hot Springs.

A cowboy statue in Wall Drug, the world's largest drugstore

A rider at the Fort Pierre rodeo

Pierre and Fort Pierre were named for fur-trader Pierre Chouteau, Jr.

An exhibit at the Enchanted World Doll Museum in Mitchell

They can view petrified trees and dinosaur tracks. Fossils of saber-toothed tigers can also be seen.

Pierre is northeast of Kadoka. It is near the state's center. Pierre has been South Dakota's capital since 1889. South Dakota's lawmakers meet in the State Capitol there. The South Dakota Cultural Heritage Center is in Pierre, too. The plate buried more than 250 years ago by the La Vérendrye brothers is there. Across the Missouri River in Fort Pierre stands the Vérendrye Monument. It marks the spot where young Hattie Foster found the plate in 1913. Each year, Fort Pierre hosts a big rodeo. It recalls South Dakota's cowboy past. Chamberlain is southeast of Pierre. The Akta Lakota Museum there shows everyday life of the early Sioux. Buffalo-hair dolls are a special exhibit.

Mitchell is east of Chamberlain. It is home to the Corn Palace. Each year, a new mural graces the building's outside walls. The pictures are made completely of colored corn and grasses. Across from the Corn Palace is the Enchanted World Doll Museum. The building looks like a castle. More than 4,000 dolls from around the world are displayed inside. The Prehistoric Indian Village is also in Mitchell. There, the remains of a 1,000-year-old Indian village are being dug up.

44

Yankton is to the southeast. It is on the Missouri River along the Nebraska border. Yankton was the Dakota Territory capital from 1861 to 1883. The territorial legislative building still stands there. Today, it is part of the Dakota Territorial Museum. The museum also includes a country schoolhouse and a blacksmith shop.

Farther southeast is Vermillion. It's a good place to end a South Dakota tour. The University of South Dakota is there. This school has the country's only museum just for musical instruments. More than 5,000 instruments are at the Shrine to Music Museum.

The Corn Palace, in Mitchell

Overleaf: Sitting Bull

45

A Gallery of Famous South Dakotans

A GALLERY OF FAMOUS SOUTH DAKOTANS

South Dakota has been home to many great people. They include Indian leaders, athletes, artists, and authors.

Sitting Bull (1831-1890) was born near present-day Bullhead. In his youth, he was a great Sioux warrior. Later, he became a medicine man and religious leader. He wanted to recover the Black Hills. Sitting Bull helped plan the Battle of the Little Bighorn (1876). The Sioux leader spent his last years on the Standing Rock Reservation. In 1890, the government feared that he would lead another uprising. Indian police came to arrest him. There was a fight and Sitting Bull was killed.

Gall (1840-1894) was born along South Dakota's Moreau River. After Gall's parents died, Sitting Bull raised him as a younger brother. Gall worked with Sitting Bull to recover the Black Hills. He led the Sioux at the Battle of the Little Bighorn. Gall also settled on the Standing Rock Reservation. He worked for schooling for Indian children.

James "Scotty" Philip (1857-1911) was born in Scotland. He came to the United States at age

The town of Philip, South Dakota, was named for James "Scotty" Philip (above).

Left: Gutzon Borglum
Right: Gladys Pyle

sixteen. Tales of gold brought him to South Dakota. Philip found no gold. But he started a big cattle ranch. He also feared that all the buffalo would be wiped out. Philip rounded up about 80 buffalo. He built them into a herd of nearly 1,000. Today, many of South Dakota's buffaloes are offspring of Philip's herd.

Gutzon Borglum (1867-1941) was born in Idaho. He became a portrait painter and sculptor.

Borglum spent his last fourteen years carving the giant sculpture on Mount Rushmore. Through binoculars, he would study the figures from miles away. Then, he would return to continue the carvings.

Zitkala-Sa (1876-1938) was born on South Dakota's Yankton Reservation. She is also known as Gertrude Bonnin. In 1901 she published a book called *Old Indian Legends.* Later, she worked for the Indian Citizenship Act (1924). That law gave Indians the rights of U.S. citizens. In 1926, she founded the National Council of American Indians. Zitkala-Sa was the group's president for twelve years. She also composed an Indian opera, *Sun Dance.*

Gladys Pyle (1890-1989) was born in Huron. At first, she was a teacher. In 1923, Pyle became South Dakota's first woman state legislator. In 1938, she became U.S. senator from South Dakota. Her mother, **Mamie Pyle** (1866-1949), worked for women's right to vote. In 1918, South Dakota women received the vote.

Harvey Dunn (1884-1952) was born in a sod house near De Smet. In the evening, he and his mother drew pictures. Dunn became an artist. During World War I, the U.S. government sent him

Zitkala-Sa (Gertrude Bonnin)

Ben Reifel

Hubert H. Humphrey

to France. He was to draw pictures showing the life of American soldiers. Dunn was proudest of his prairie pictures. They showed life in South Dakota. *Dakota Woman* and *After the Blizzard* are two of them.

Oscar Howe (1915-1983) was born on South Dakota's Crow Creek Reservation. As a child, he drew with charcoal from his mother's cooking fire. Howe later used geometric shapes and bright colors in his paintings. They showed Sioux values and beliefs. Howe also designed murals for the Corn Palace (1948-1971).

Ernest O. Lawrence (1901-1958) was born in Canton. He helped start the Atomic Age. In 1931, Lawrence built the first cyclotron. This machine smashes atoms. In 1939, Lawrence won the Nobel Prize in physics. Later, he played a big role in building the first atomic bomb.

Ben Reifel (1906-1990) was born on South Dakota's Rosebud Reservation. His father was a German farmer. His mother was a Sioux. Reifel served in the U.S. House of Representatives (1961-1971). At that time, he was the only American Indian in Congress.

Wallace was the birthplace of **Hubert Humphrey** (1911-1978). As a young man, he was a druggist and a teacher. Humphrey became well known as a U.S. senator from Minnesota (1949-1965 and 1971-1978). In the Senate, Humphrey helped start the Food for Peace and the Peace Corps programs. He also served as vice president of the United States (1965-1969).

George McGovern was born in Avon in 1922. He grew up in Mitchell. McGovern was a World War II bomber pilot. He won the Distinguished Flying Cross. McGovern served South Dakota in the U.S. House of Representatives (1957-1961). Then, he became a U.S. senator (1963-1981). In between, McGovern directed Food for Peace. As a senator, he spoke out against the Vietnam War.

Allen Neuharth was born in Eureka in 1924. As a boy, he delivered newspapers. Neuharth also edited his high school paper. In 1982, Neuharth began publishing *USA Today*. About 6 million people read this newspaper each day.

Many South Dakotans have become sports stars. **Earle Sande** (1898-1968) was born in Groton. He became a great jockey. Sande won the Kentucky Derby three times. **Casey Tibbs** (1929-1990) was born in Mission Ridge. He was national rodeo champion in 1951 and 1955. **Norm Van Brocklin** (1926-1983) was born in Eagle Butte. He was a great quarterback. Van Brocklin led the Los Angeles

George McGovern

Casey Tibbs

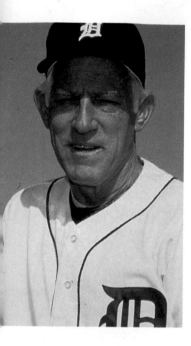

Sparky Anderson

Each year the Caldecott is awarded to the best-illustrated children's book.

Rams and Philadelphia Eagles to national championships. **George "Sparky" Anderson** was born in 1934 in Bridgewater. He is a great baseball manager. He led the Cincinnati Reds to World Series titles (1975 and 1976). In 1984, his Detroit Tigers won the World Series. **Billy Mills** was born on the Pine Ridge Reservation in 1938. In 1964, Mills won the Olympic gold medal for the 10,000-meter race. He is the only American ever to win that Olympic event.

Vine Deloria, Jr., was born in Martin in 1933. He grew up on the nearby Pine Ridge Reservation. Deloria wrote about his people, the Sioux. *Custer Died for Your Sins* is one of his books. Deloria also wrote a children's book. *Native American Animal Stories* was published in 1992.

Paul Goble was born in England in 1933. He moved to South Dakota's Black Hills in the 1970s. Goble retells Indian stories for children. He also illustrates them. *The Girl Who Loved Wild Horses* won the 1979 Caldecott Medal.

More than 10 million viewers get the news from a South Dakotan. **Tom Brokaw** was born in Webster in 1940. He worked in radio during high school and college. Since 1982, Brokaw has anchored NBC television's nightly news.

The birthplace of Tom Brokaw, Billy Mills, *Tom Brokaw*
Gladys Pyle, Zitkala-Sa, and Hubert Humphrey . . .

Home, too, of Scotty Philip, Gutzon Borglum, and Paul Goble . . .

The site of Mount Rushmore, the Corn Palace, and the world's oldest continuously worked gold mine . . .

The state that ranks first in growing oats and rye, and that has the most buffaloes . . .

This is the Sunshine State—South Dakota!

Did You Know?

Calamity Jane came to Deadwood in 1875 disguised as a soldier. Her real name was Martha Jane Cannary Burke. During an outbreak of smallpox in 1878, she nursed Deadwood's sick miners.

James Fraser of Mitchell designed the buffalo nickel. The Indian head on the front of the coin was that of a South Dakotan. He was the distinguished Rosebud tribal leader Hollow Horn Bear. More than 1 billion of those nickels were minted from 1913 to 1938.

A billion pounds of rock were removed to build the Mount Rushmore Memorial. Most of the rock was blown away by dynamite.

The 1990 Academy Award-winning movie *Dances With Wolves* was filmed in South Dakota. The final scene of the 1959 film *North by Northwest* takes place atop Mount Rushmore.

Tea, a town near Sioux Falls, was nearly named Beer. Other oddly named South Dakota towns include Porcupine, Badger, Whitehorse, and Winner.

In 1990, South Dakota renamed its Columbus Day holiday "Native American Day." Instead of honoring Columbus, South Dakotans now honor American Indians.

James Witherspoon, an early Yankton farmer, reportedly walked 1,200 miles to Washington, D.C., to obtain his land title.

The town of Brookings was named for Judge W. W. Brookings. During his first winter in South Dakota (1857-1858), his legs froze so badly that they had to be amputated. Brookings went on to become a South Dakota Supreme Court judge.

In 1905, Amanda Clement of Hudson became the first official woman umpire in baseball.

Hundreds of wild mustangs run free near Hot Springs at the Black Hills Wild Horse Sanctuary.

In 1993, eighty-five tornadoes struck South Dakota. Only Texas and Kansas had more.

More than 10,000 duckbilled dinosaurs lie buried in Ziebach County. They died mysteriously about 65 million years ago.

A father and son, George T. Mickelson and George S. Mickelson, both served as governors of South Dakota.

On November 11, 1935, Albert Stevens and Orvil Anderson took off in a balloon near Rapid City. Their eight-hour flight reached a height of 72,395 feet (nearly 14 miles) before landing 240 miles to the east.

Published by
RISE STUDIO
807

Con:
Nati
—U.
Stra
Rap

South Dakota Information

Area: 77,116 square miles (the sixteenth-biggest state)

Greatest Distance North to South: 237 miles

Greatest Distance East to West: 383 miles

Borders: North Dakota to the north; Minnesota and Iowa to the east; Nebraska to the south; Wyoming and Montana to the west

Highest Point: Harney Peak in the Black Hills, 7,242 feet above sea level

Lowest Point: Big Stone Lake in the northeast, 966 feet above sea level

Hottest Recorded Temperature: 120° F. (at Gannvalley, on July 5, 1936)

Coldest Recorded Temperature: -58° F. (at McIntosh, on February 17, 1936)

Statehood: The fortieth state, on November 2, 1889

Origin of Name: South Dakota was named for the Dakota, or Sioux, Indians; the word *Dakota* means "friends" in the Sioux language

Capital: Pierre

Counties: 66

United States Representatives: 1

State Senators: 35

State Representatives: 70

State Song: "Hail, South Dakota," by Deecort Hammitt

State Motto: "Under God the People Rule"

Nicknames: "Sunshine State," "Coyote State," "Land of Infinite Variety," "Blizzard State," "Mount Rushmore State"

State Seal: Adopted in 1889

State Flag: Adopted in 1992

State Flower: American pasqueflower
State Tree: Black Hills spruce
State Grass: Western wheatgrass
State Bird: Ring-necked pheasant
State Mineral Stone: Rose quartz
State Gemstone: Fairburn agate
State Musical Instrument: Fiddle
State Colors: Blue and gold

State Animal: Coyote
State Insect: Honeybee
State Fish: Walleye
State Fossil: Triceratops
State Drink: Milk

Ring-necked pheasant

Some Rivers: Missouri, Big Sioux, James, Grand, Moreau, Cheyenne, White

Some Lakes: Oahe, Francis Case, Sharpe, Lewis and Clark, Medicine, Waubay, Big Stone, Traverse

Wildlife: Buffalo, coyotes, bighorn sheep, Rocky Mountain goats, porcupines, bobcats, pronghorns, prairie dogs, badgers, deer, elk, foxes, skunks, gophers, squirrels, black bears, rattlesnakes, ring-necked pheasants, eagles, geese, ducks, swans, wild turkeys, owls, many other kinds of birds, walleyes, northern pike, bass, bluegills, trout, paddlefish, many other kinds of fish

Manufactured Products: Meat, animal feed, and other packaged foods, seeding equipment, grain elevators, other machinery, jewelry, medical instruments, hot-air balloons

Farm Products: Oats, rye, honey, hay, barley, wheat, sorghum, soybeans, corn, sunflower seeds, flaxseed, beef cattle, sheep, lambs, hogs, turkeys, milk, eggs

Mining Products: Gold, oil, natural gas, mica, granite, crushed stone, sand and gravel, clays

Population: 696,004, forty-fifth among the states (1990 U.S. Census Bureau figures)

Coyote

Rose quartz

Major Cities (1990 Census):

Sioux Falls	100,814	Mitchell	13,798
Rapid City	54,523	Pierre	12,906
Aberdeen	24,927	Yankton	12,703
Watertown	17,592	Huron	12,448
Brookings	16,270	Vermillion	10,034

SOUTH DAKOTA HISTORY

These Deadwood Central Railroad Engineer Corps surveyors were planning a railroad.

8000 B.C.—The first people reach South Dakota

1682—La Salle claims land in North America, including present-day South Dakota, for France

1700s—Arikara, Cheyenne, and Sioux Indians are established in South Dakota

1743—François and Louis-Joseph La Vérendrye become the first known white explorers in South Dakota

1762—France gives its land west of the Mississippi River, including South Dakota, to Spain

1800—France regains its western lands from Spain

1803—France sells its western lands to the United States

1804—Meriwether Lewis and William Clark explore South Dakota on their way to the Pacific Ocean

1817—Joseph La Framboise begins South Dakota's first permanent non-Indian settlement, at present-day Fort Pierre

1861—The United States government forms the Dakota Territory

1862—The United States government passes the Homestead Act, which offers free land to settlers

1868—Red Cloud's War ends with the signing of the Fort Laramie Treaty; the Sioux are promised the Black Hills

1872—The first railroad begins operating in South Dakota

1874—George Custer's expedition finds gold in the Black Hills

1876—Thousands of miners pour into the Black Hills in search of gold

1877—The United States government officially takes the Black Hills from the Sioux

1888—South Dakota is hit by the Great Blizzard, which kills dozens of people

1889—South Dakota becomes the fortieth state on November 2

1890—United States soldiers kill 300 Sioux Indians, including many women and children, at Wounded Knee Creek

1897—An eight-year drought ends in South Dakota

1910—The present-day State Capitol opens at Pierre

1917-18—About 32,000 South Dakotans help win World War I

1927—Gutzon Borglum begins the Mount Rushmore National Memorial

1929-39—The Great Depression hits the United States; drought and dust storms make life even harder for South Dakotans

1941—Work ends on the Mount Rushmore National Memorial

1941-45—More than 64,000 South Dakotans help win World War II

1944-66—Through the Pick-Sloan Missouri Basin Program, four dams are built on the Missouri River

1964—Hubert H. Humphrey is elected vice president of the United States

1972—Rapid City's Canyon Lake Dam collapses, killing at least 236 people

1973—Indians seize the site of Wounded Knee and hold it for seventy-one days to protest the government's treatment of American Indians

1979—The United States Court of Claims orders the United States government to pay the Sioux over $100 million for land seized in the Black Hills in 1877

1987—South Dakota's state lottery begins

1988—South Dakota legalizes gambling; National Indian Gaming Act authorizes tribal casinos

1989—Happy 100th birthday, South Dakota!

1990—The Sunshine State's population is 696,004

1993—A plane crash kills Governor George S. Mickelson; the Midwest floods cause seven deaths and $726 million in crop damage

1994—William J. Janklow is elected governor

This wagon was part of the 1989 Centennial wagon train that celebrated South Dakota's 100th birthday.

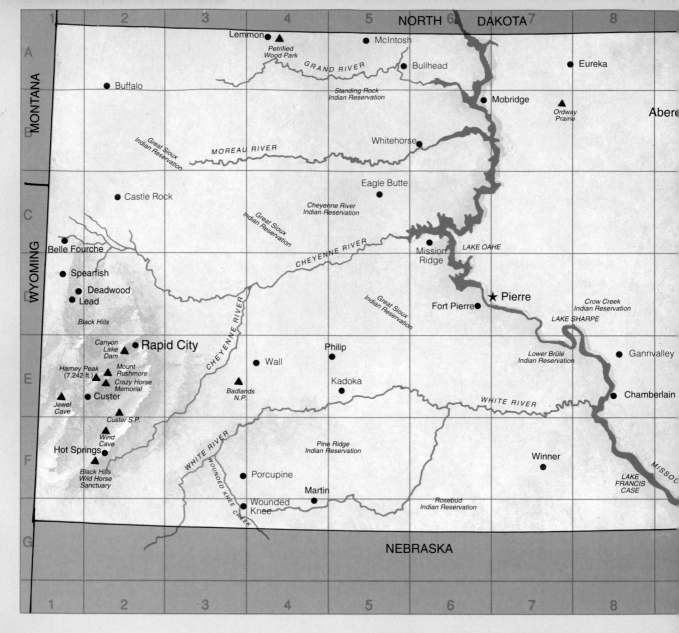

MAP KEY

	Canton	F12	Gannvalley	E8	Lemmon	A4
	Canyon Lake Dam	E2	Grand River	A4,5	Lewis and Clark Lake	G10,11
	Castle Rock	C2	Great Sioux Indian		Lower Brulé
Aberdeen B9	Chamberlain	E8	Reservation	B,C,D2,3,4,5	Indian Reservation	E7
Avon G10	Cheyenne River	D4,5	Groton	B10	Madison	E11
Badger D11	Cheyenne River		Harney Peak	E2	Martin	F4
Badlands	Indian Reservation	C4,5	Hot Springs	F2	McIntosh	A5
National Park E3	Crazy Horse Memorial	E2	Hudson	F12	Milbank	B12
Belle Fourche C1	Crow Creek		Huron	D9	Mission Ridge	C6
Big Sioux River F,G12	Indian Reservation	D8	James River	D,E10	Missouri River	F9
Big Stone Lake B12	Custer	E2	Jewel Cave	E1	Mitchell	E10
Black Hills D1,2	Custer State Park	F2	Kadoka	E5	Mobridge	B6
Black Hills	Deadwood	D2	Lake Francis Case	F8	Moreau River	B3,4
Wild Horse Sanctuary F2	De Smet	D10	Lake Kampeska	C11	Mount Rushmore	E2
Bridgewater F11	Devil's Gulch	E12	Lake Oahe	C6	Ordway Prairie	B7
Brookings D12	Eagle Butte	C5	Lake Sharpe	D7,8	Palisades State Park	E12
Buffalo A2	Eureka	A8	Lake Traverse	A12	Pelican Lake	C11
Bullhead A5	Fort Pierre	D6	Lead	D1	Petrified Wood Park	A4

Philip	E5	Wall	E4
Pierre	D7	Wallace	B11
Pine Ridge		Watertown	C11
Indian Reservation	F4,5	Waubay Lake	B11
Porcupine	F4	Waubay National	
Rapid City	E2	Wildlife Refuge	B11
Rosebud		Webster	B10
Indian Reservation	G6	Wentworth	E12
Roy Lake	A11	Whitehorse	B6
Sioux Falls	F12	White River	F3;E6,7
Sisseton	A11	White Rock	A12
Sisseton		Wind Cave	F2
Indian Reservation	A11	Winner	F7
Spearfish	D1	Wounded Knee	G4
Standing Rock		Wounded Knee Creek	F,G3
Indian Reservation	A,B5	Yankton	G11
Tea	F12	Yankton	
Vermillion	G12	Indian Reservation	G10,11

GLOSSARY

ancient: Relating to a time long ago in history

billion: A thousand million (1,000,000,000)

blizzard: A snowstorm driven by very strong winds

butte: A flat-topped mountain or hill that rises sharply above the nearby land

canyon: A deep, steep-sided valley

capital: The city that is the seat of government

capitol: The building in which the government meets

century: A period of 100 years

climate: The typical weather of a region

drought: A period when rainfall is well below normal

expedition: A journey usually made to learn information about new places

explorer: A person who visits and studies unknown lands

homesteader: A person who receives ownership of land by living on it and improving it

61

million: A thousand thousand (1,000,000)

mustang: A small Great Plains horse

plains: Generally flat lands

population: The number of people in a place

posse: A group usually organized by a sheriff to capture an outlaw

prairie: Grassland

rodeo: An event at which cowboys and cowgirls compete at riding and roping

sod house: A home built with chunks of ground dug from the prairie

territory: The name of a part of the United States before it becomes a state

tornado: A powerful windstorm that comes from a whirling, funnel-shaped cloud

tourism: The business of providing services such as lodging and food for visitors

wildlife refuge: A place where animals are protected

PICTURE ACKNOWLEDGMENTS

Front cover, ©SuperStock; 1, ©Chuck Pefley/Tony Stone Images, Inc.; 2, Tom Dunnington; 3, ©Pat Wadecki/Root Resources; 4-5, Tom Dunnington; 6-7, ©Roger Bickel/N E Stock Photo; 8, ©T. Dietrich/H. Armstrong Roberts; 9 (left), ©Tom Till; 9 (right), Courtesy of Hammond Incorporated, Maplewood, New Jersey; 10 (top), ©Rod Planck/Dembinsky Photo Assoc; 10 (bottom), ©David W. Middleton/SuperStock; 11, ©Rod Planck/Dembinsky Photo Assoc.; 12-13, South Dakota Art Museum Collection, Brookings, S.D.; 14, ©Reinhard Brucker; 15, South Dakota State Historical Society—State Archives; 17, S.D. State Hist. Soc.—State Arch.; 19 (top), ©H. Schmeiser/N E Stock Photo; 19 (bottom), North Wind Picture Archives; 20, S.D. State Hist. Soc.—State Arch.; 21 (both pictures), The Bettmann Archive; 22, UPI/Bettmann; 23, The Bettmann Archive; 24, UPI/Bettmann; 25, ©Gene Ahrens; 27, ©Mike Roemer; 28, S.D. Tourism/Chad Coppess Photo; 29 (top), South Dakota Tourism; 29 (bottom), ©Paul Horsted; 30 (left), ©K. Eilbeck; 30 (right), ©Randall B. Henne/Dembinski Photo Assoc.; 31, ©Paul Horsted; 32-33, ©Tom Dietrich; 34, ©Mike Roemer; 35, ©Lani Howe/Photri, Inc.; 36, ©Bill Howe/Photri, Inc.; 37, ©Bill Howe/Photri, Inc.; 38, ©Mike Roemer; 39, ©Susan Malis/mga/Photri; 40 (left), ©Mark E. Gibson/mga/Photri; 40 (right), ©Pat Wadecki/Root Resources; 41 (top), S.D.Tourism/photo by Tim Schoon; 41 (bottom), ©Pat Wadecki/Root Resources; 42 ©Bill Ross/Tony Stone Images, Inc.; 43 (top), ©Reinhard Brucker; 43 (bottom), ©Bill Ross/H. Armstrong Roberts; 44 (top), S.D. Tourism, photo by Tim Schoon; 44 (bottom), S. D. Tourism/D.J.A.; 45, ©Reinhard Brucker; 46, S. D. State Hist. Soc.—State Arch.; 47, S.D. State Hist. Soc.—State Arch.; 48 (both pictures), S.D. State Hist. Soc.—State Arch.; 49, S.D. State Hist. Soc.—State Arch.; 50 (top), S.D. State Hist. Soc.—State Arch.; 50 (bottom), Wide World Photos, Inc.; 51 (top), UPI/Bettmann; 51 (bottom), AP/Wide World Photos; 52, Bettmann; 53, Wide World Photos, Inc.; 54 (top), Courtesy of the American Numismatic Association; 54 (bottom), Buffalo Bill Historical Center; 55 (top), Courtesy of the American Numismatic Association; 55 (bottom), S.D. State Hist. Soc.—State Arch.; 56 (top), Courtesy Flag Research Center, Winchester, Massachusetts, 01890; 56 (bottom), ©John Kohout/Root Resources; 57 (top), ©Ted Rose/N E Stock Photo; 57 (middle and bottom), ©Reinhard Brucker; 58, Library of Congress; 59, ©Jerry Hennen; 60-61, Tom Dunnington; back cover, ©Bob Thomason/Tony Stone Images, Inc.

Index

Page numbers in boldface type indicate illustrations.

Aberdeen, 29-30, 37-38, **38**, 57
Adams Memorial Museum, 41
agriculture, 4, 23-24, **24**, 26, 27, **27**,
  30-31, **30**, 57
Akta Lakota Museum, 44
American Indians, 14-15, **15**, 19-20,
  19, 21-23, 26, 27, 29, 58
Anderson, George "Sparky," 52, **52**
Anderson, Orvil, 55, **55**
Arikara Indians, 14-15, 58
Badger, 54
Badlands, 8, **8**, **11**, 34
Badlands National Park, 43, **back cover**
Badlands Petrified Gardens, 43-44
Battle of the Little Bighorn, 21, 47
Battle of Slim Buttes, 22
Baum, L. Frank, 38
Belle Fourche, 39-40
Big Foot, 23
Big Sioux River, **6-7**, 9, **9**, 34, 57
Big Stone Lake, 8-9, 56, 57
birds, 10, **10**, 57, **57**
Black Hills, 4, 8, 10, 15, 20, 22, 24,
  31, 34, 40, 41, 43, 47, 58, 59
Black Hills Mining Museum, 40
Black Hills Rodeo, **29**
Black Hills Wild Horse Sanctuary, 55
Bonnin, Gertrude. *See* Zitkala-Sa.
borders, 8, 56
Borglum, Gutzon, 48-49, **48**, 59
Brokaw, Tom, 52, **53**
Brookings, 35-36, **36**, 55, 57
Brookings, W. W., 55
Buffalo, 39
Calamity Jane (Martha Jane Cannary
  Burke), 4, 41, 54, **54**
Canyon Lake Dam, 11, 59
capital. *See* Pierre
Case Lake, 9, 57
Castle Rock, 39
Center of the Nation Visitor Center, 39
Chamberlain, 44
Cheyenne Indians, 14, 15, 58
Cheyenne River, 9, 57

Cheyenne River Reservation, 38
Chouteau, Pierre, Jr., 17, 18
Clark, William, 4, 17, 58
Clement, Amanda, 55
climate, 10-11, **11**, 23, **24**, 26, 55,
  56, 58, 59
Corn Palace, 44, **45**, 50
Crazy Horse, 4, 21, 22
Crazy Horse Memorial, **28**, 42, **42**
Crow Creek Reservation, 50
Custer, George, 20, 21, 58
Custer State Park, **3**, 42-43
Dakota Territorial Museum, 45
Dakota Territory, 18, 58
Deadwood, 20, 21, **21**, 25-26, 40-41,
  41, 54
Deloria, Vine, Jr., 52
De Smet, 36-37, **37**, 49
Devil's Gulch, 34-35
dinosaurs, 14, **14**, 39, 41, 44, 55
Dorion, Pierre, 16
Dunn, Harvey, 36, 49-50
  painting by, **12-13**
Eagle Butte, 38
employment, 24, 29-31
Enchanted World Doll Museum, 44, **44**
fish, 10, 37, 57
Fort Laramie Treaty, 58
Fort Pierre, 16, 17, **17**, 18, 44, **44**, 58
Fort Pierre National Grasslands, **1**
Foss, Joe, 25
Foster, Hattie, 44
Fraser, James, 54
Gall, 21, **21**, 47
gambling, 26, 27, 59
Gannvalley, 56
Gavins Point Dam, **25**
Goble, Paul, 52
gold, 4, 20, 24, 31, 58
Grand River, 9, 57
Great Dakota Bust, 23
Great Depression, 24, 59
Great Lakes of South Dakota, 9, 25
Great Plains, 8

Great Plains Zoo, 34, **34**
Harney Peak, 8, 42-43, 56
Harrison, Benjamin, 23, 23
history, 14-27, 58-59
Homestake Gold Mine, 40, **40**
Homestead Act (1862), 18, 58
homesteaders, 18-19, **19**
Hot Springs, 43, **43**, 55
Howe, Oscar, 36, 38, 50
Humphrey, Hubert H., 50-51, **50**, 59
Huron, 57
Indian Citizenship Act (1924), 49
industry, 57
Iowa, 8, 56
James, Jesse, 34-35
James River, 9, 57
Jefferson, Thomas, 17, 42
Jewel Cave, 43
Kadoka, 43, 44
La Framboise, Joseph, 17, 58
Lake Francis Case, 9, 57
Lake Kampeska, 37
Lake Oahe, 9, 57
Lake Sharpe, 9, 57
Lake Traverse, 9, 57
lakes, 8-9, 37
Laramie Treaty, 19
La Salle, René-Robert Cavelier, Sieur
  de, 16, 58
La Vérendrye, François, 16, 44, 58
La Vérendrye, Louis-Joseph, 16, 44, 58
Lawrence, Ernest O., 50
Lead, 20, 40, **40**
Lemmon, 38, 39
Lewis, Meriwether, 4, 17, 58
Lewis and Clark Lake, 9, **25**, 57
Lincoln, Abraham, 42
Madison, 35
Mammoth Site, 43, **43**
maps of South Dakota showing:
  cities and geographical features, **60-61**
  location in U. S., **2**
  products and history, **4-5**
  topography, **9**

McCall, Jack, 21
McCrory Gardens, 36
McGovern, George, 51, **51**
McIntosh, 56
Medicine Lake, 57
Mellette, Arthur, 23
Mellette House, 37
Mickelson, George S., 27, 55, 59
Mickelson, George T., 55
Milbank Lake, 37
Mills, Billy, 52
mining, 19, 31, 57
Minnesota, 8, 56
Missouri River, 9, 14, 17, 18, 25, 44, 45, 57, 59
Mitchell, 44, **44, 45,** 54, 57
Mobridge, 38
Montana, 8, 18, 19, 40, 56
Moreau River, 9, 47, 57
Mount Moriah Cemetery, 41
Mount Rushmore, **32-33,** 41-42, 49, 54, 59
Museum of Geology, **14,** 41
Music Museum, 45
National Council of American Indians, 49
National Indian Gaming Act (1988), 59
Native American Day, 54
Nebraska, 56
Neuharth, Allen, 51
nicknames, South Dakota's 4, 8, 10, 30
North Dakota, 8, 18, 23, 56
Ordway Prairie, 38
Pacific Ocean, 16
Palisades State Park, 9, 35
Pelican Lake, 37
Petrified Wood Park, 38, **39**

Pettigrew, Richard, 34
Philip, James "Scotty," 47-48, **47**
Pick-Sloan Missouri Basin Program, 25, 59
Pierre, 23, 44, 56, 57, 59, **front cover**
Pine Ridge Reservation, 26
plants, 10, **56,** 57
population, 25, 29, 57, 59
Porcupine, 54
Prairie Village, 35
Prehistoric Indian Village, 44
Pyle, Gladys, **48,** 49
Pyle, Mamie, 49
railroads, 19, 22, 58, **58**
Rapid City, 11, 25, **30,** 41, 57, 59
Red Cloud, 19, **19,** 58
Reifel, Ben, 50, **50**
rivers, 9, 57
Rocky Mountains, 8
Roosevelt, Theodore, 42
Rosebud Indians, 54
Rosebud Reservation, 50
Roy Lake, 37
Sande, Earle, 51
Scherr-Howe Arena, 38
Self-Determination Act for Native Americans (1975), 26
Sioux Cultural Center, 38
Sioux Falls, 18, 25, 27, 30, 31, 34, **35,** 54, 57
Sioux Indians, 4, 14, 15, 15, 16, 18, 19-23, **22,** 26, **28,** 29, 37, 38, 50, 56, 58, 59
Siouxland Heritage Museums, 34
Sisseton, 37
Sitting Bull, 4, 21, 22-23, 38, **46,** 47
South Dakota Art Museum, 36
South Dakota Cultural Heritage

Center, 44
Standing Rock Reservation, 38, 47
State Agricultural Heritage Museum, 36, **36**
state symbols, 10, 56-57, **56, 57**
Stevens, Albert, 55, 55
Storybook Land, 37-38, **38**
Tea, 54
Tekakwitha Fine Arts Center, 37
Tibbs, Casey, 51, **51**
Tri-State Museum, 39-40
Van Brocklin, Norm, 51-52
Vérendrye Monument, 44
Vermillion, 45, 57
Vermillion River, 9
Wall, 43-44, **43**
Washington, George, 42
Watertown, 37, 57
Waubay Lake, 57
Whitehorse, 54
White River, 9, 57
Wild Bill Hickok, 4, 21, 41, **41**
Wilder, Laura Ingalls, 36-37, **37**
Wilder, Laura Ingalls, Pageant, 37
wildlife, 3, 10, **10,** 38, 42, 43, 48, 57, **57**
Wind Cave, 43
Winner, 54
Witherspoon, James, 55
World War I, 24, 49-50, 59
World War II, 24-25, 59
Wounded Knee, 26, 59
Wounded Knee Creek, **22,** 23, 59
Wylie Park, 37
Wyoming, 8, 18, 19, 40, 56
Yankton, 16, 18, 45, 57
Ziolkowski, Korczak, 42
Zitkala-Sa, 49, **49**

ABOUT THE AUTHORS

Dennis and Judith Fradin have coauthored several books in the From Sea to Shining Sea series. The Fradins both graduated from Northwestern University in 1967. Dennis has been a professional writer for twenty years, and has published 150 books. His works for Childrens Press include the Young People's Stories of Our States series, the Disaster! series, and the Thirteen Colonies series. Judith earned her M.A. in literature from Northwestern University and taught high-school and college English for many years. The Fradins, who are the parents of Anthony, Diana, and Michael, live in Evanston, Illinois.